Growing Readers
New Hanover County Public Library
Purchased with
New Hanover County Partnership for Children
and Smart Start Funds

DOCTORS HELP PEOPLE

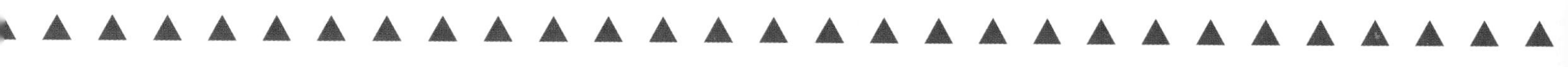

Design and electronic page composition
Lindaanne Donohoe Design

Photo research
Feldman & Associates, Inc.

Picture Acknowledgments

©**SuperStock International, Inc.** — Cover, 3, 4, 5, 6, 7, 8, 10, 11, 12, 13, 15, 17, 19, 20, 23, 24, 25, 26, 27, 28, 30

©**Blair Seitz** — 9, 14, 16, 21, 22, 29

©**Doug Plummer** — 18

PhotoEdit — ©Shelley Boyd — 23

Library of Congress Cataloging-in-Publication Data

Moses, Amy.

Doctors help people. / Amy Moses.
p. cm.
Includes index.
Summary: Discusses, simply, the things doctors do and what people do to become doctors.
ISBN 1-56766-304-4 (hardcover)
1. Physicians — Juvenile literature.
2. Medicine — Vocational guidance — Juvenile literature.
[1. Physicians. 2. Medicine — Vocational guidance. 3. Vocational guidance.]
I. Title.

R690.M596 1996 96-5241
610.69'52—dc20 CIP
AC

DOCTORS HELP PEOPLE

By Amy Moses

THE CHILD'S WORLD®

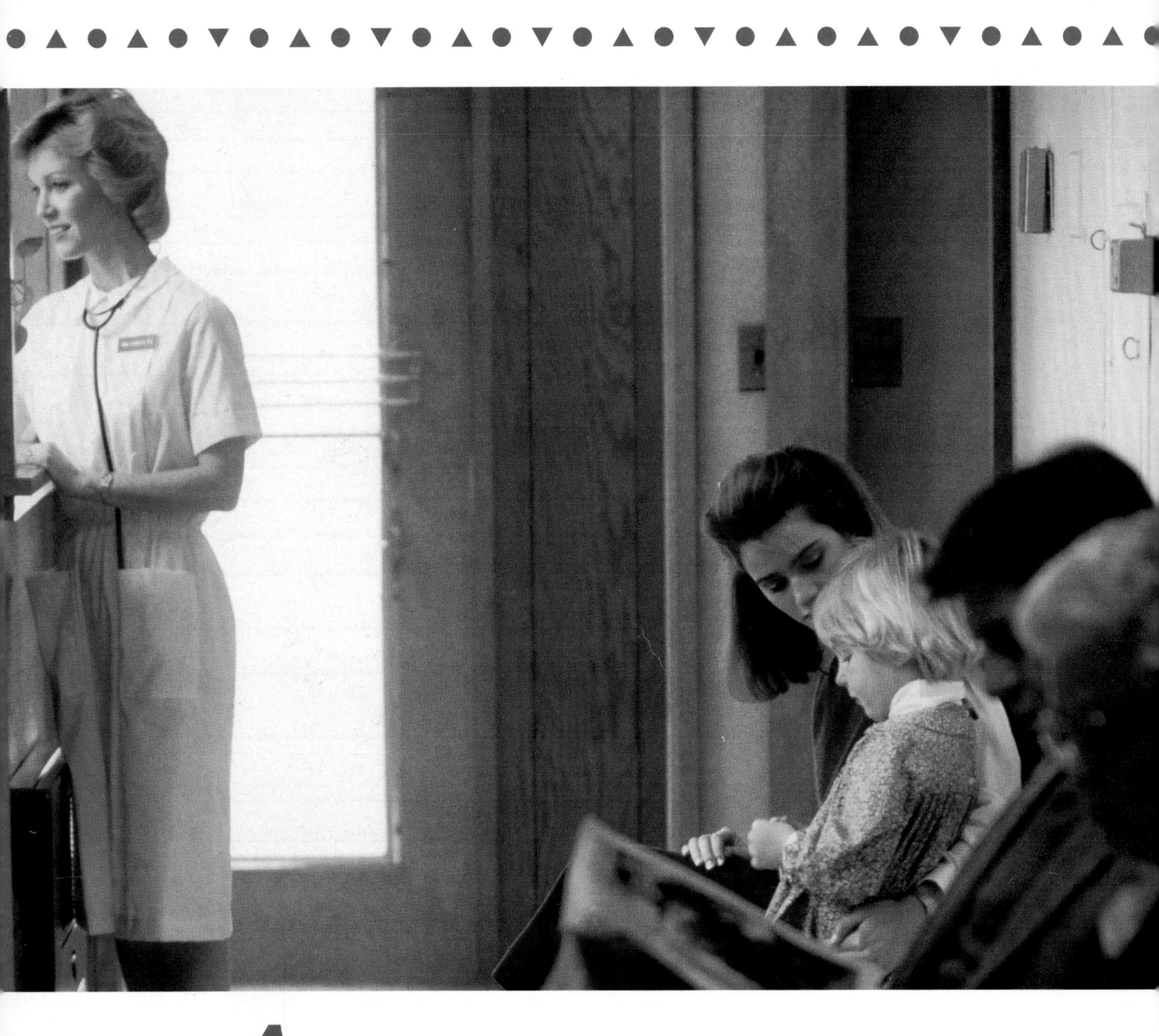

Achoo-achoo! Cough-Cough! Sniffle-Sniffle! It's the cold and flu season, for sure! These people are sick. They are waiting to see the doctor.

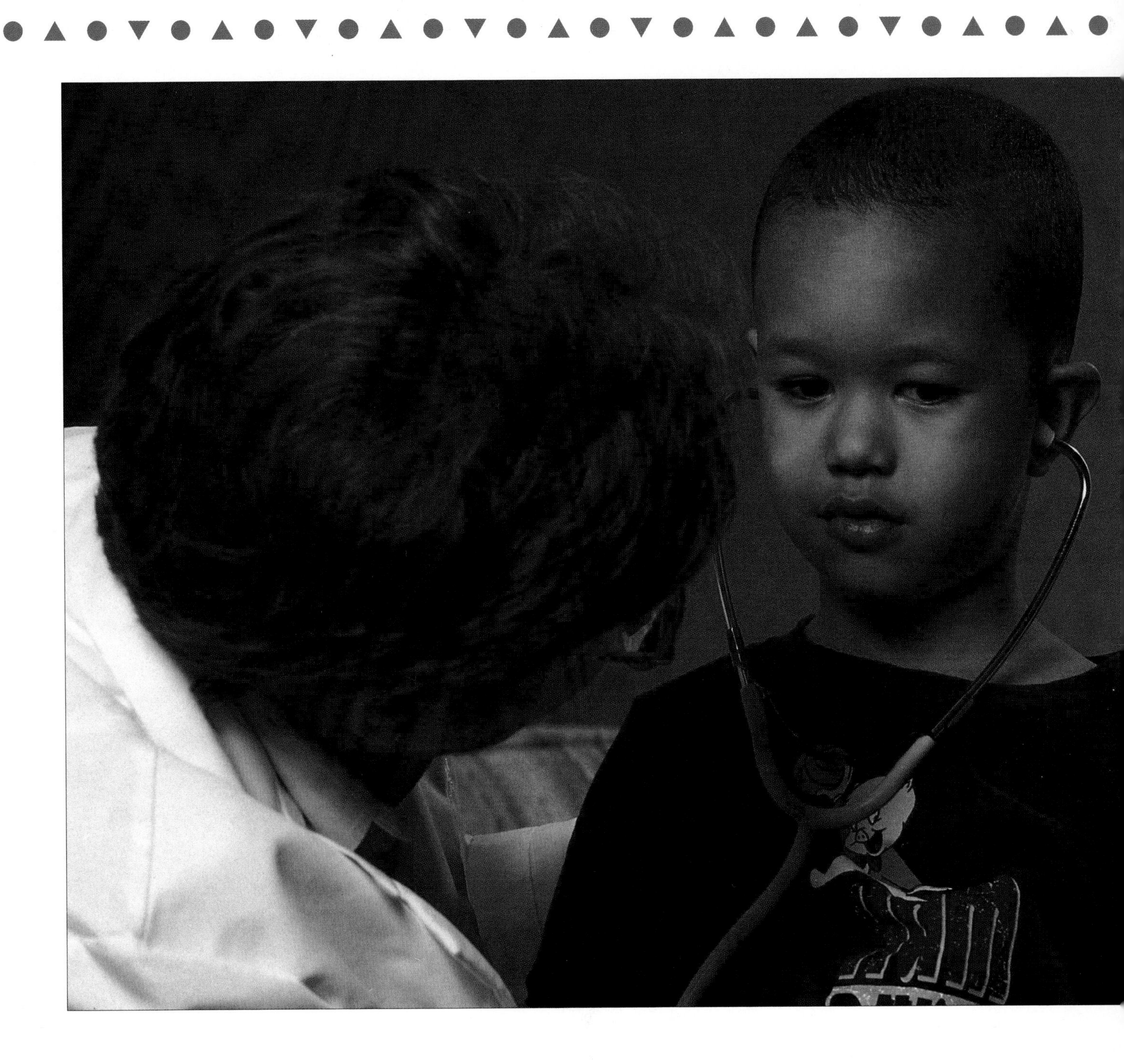

Someone has an earache.
Someone else has a sore throat.
This boy is visiting the doctor because he does not feel well.

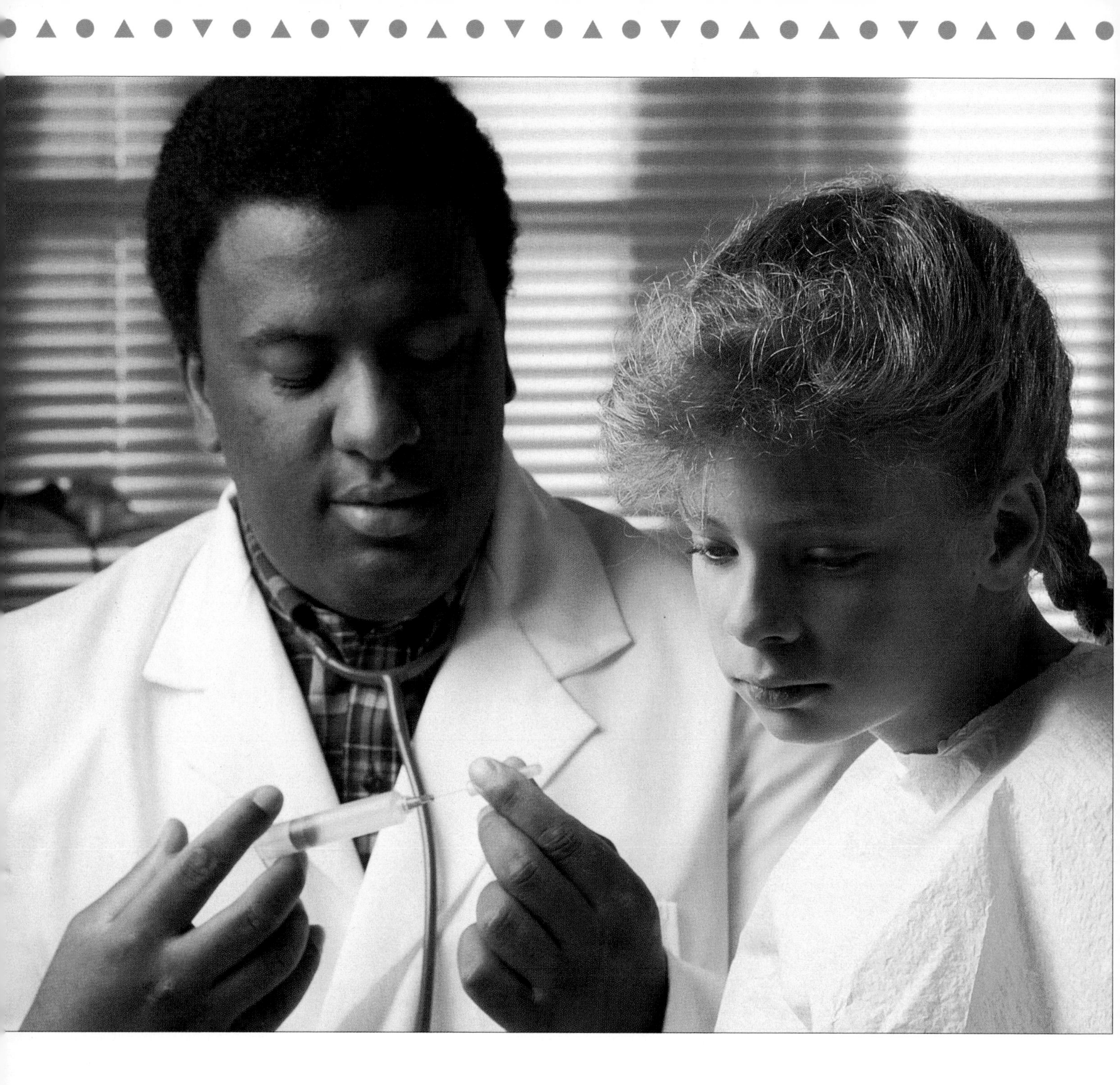

This girl is here for a checkup and a shot.
When was the last time you had
a checkup or a shot?

This doctor is a pediatrician—
a doctor who takes care of children.
Your pediatrician wants you to feel good.

By giving you a checkup, your doctor makes sure your body is strong and healthy.

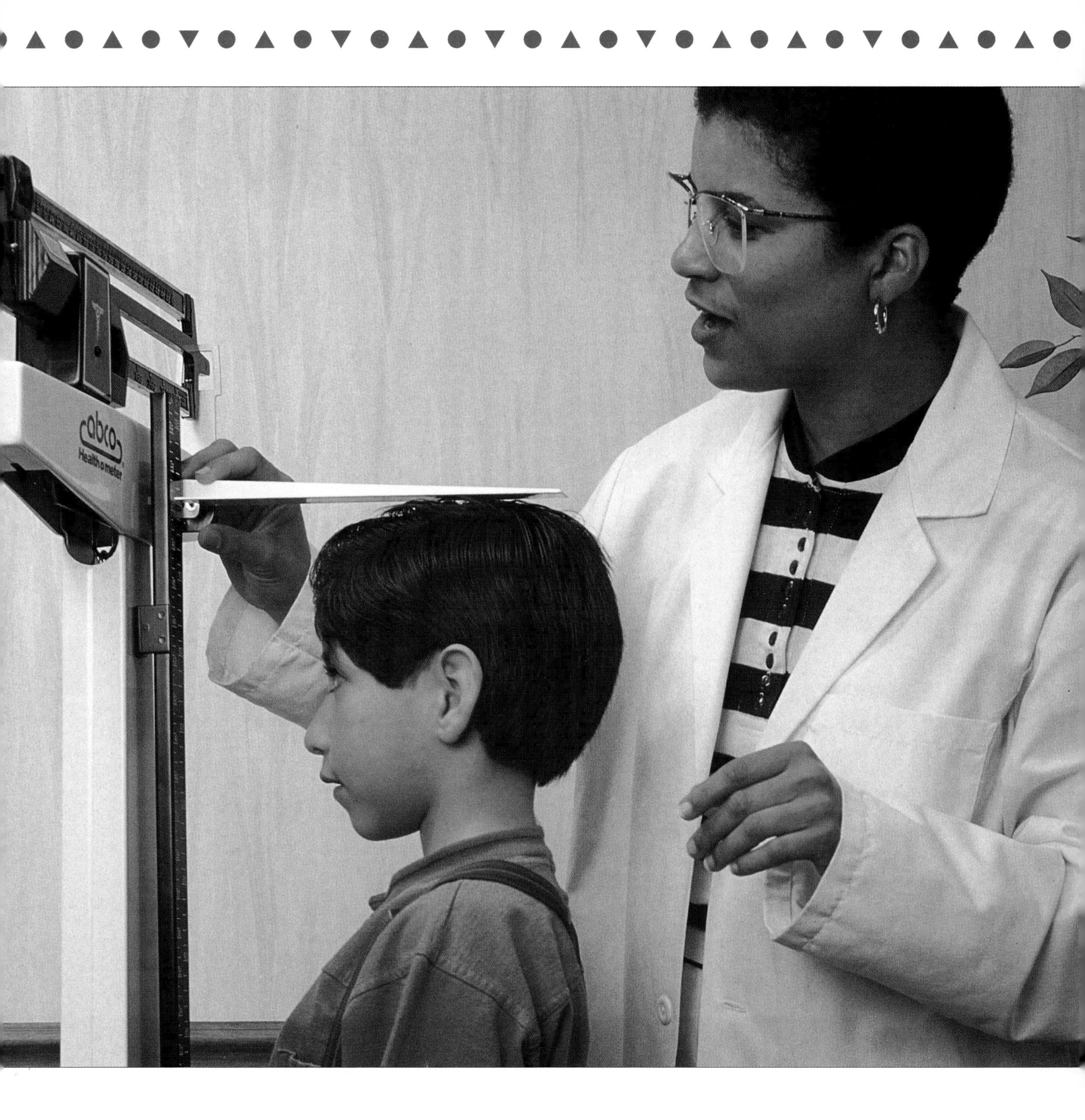

Are you growing? Step up on the scale.
Now your doctor can weigh and measure you.

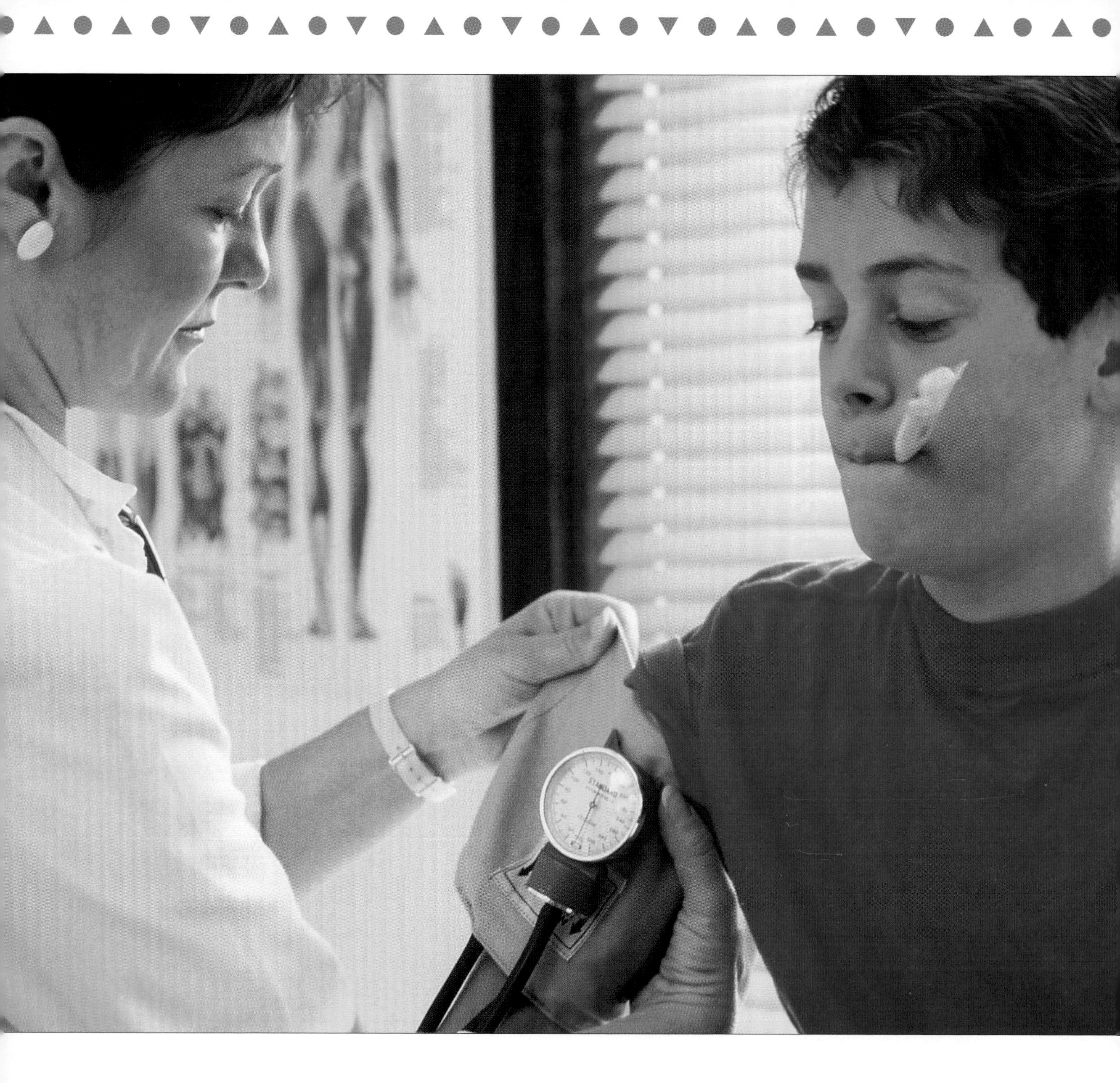

The doctor asks you some questions.
Then she takes your temperature.
She measures your blood pressure too.

Your blood pressure tells the doctor how well your heart is pumping blood through your body.

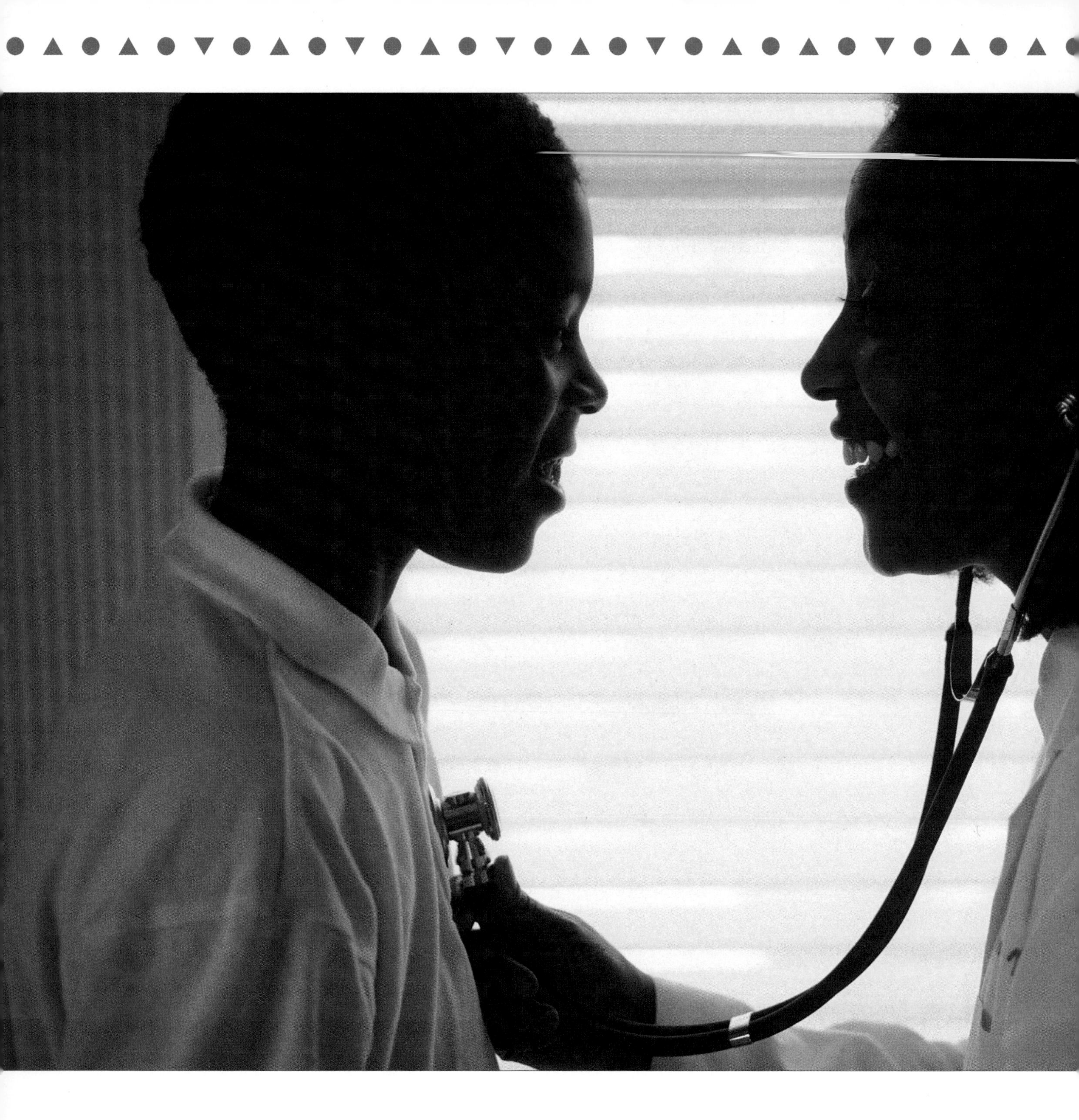

Your doctor listens to the sounds in your body with a stethoscope.

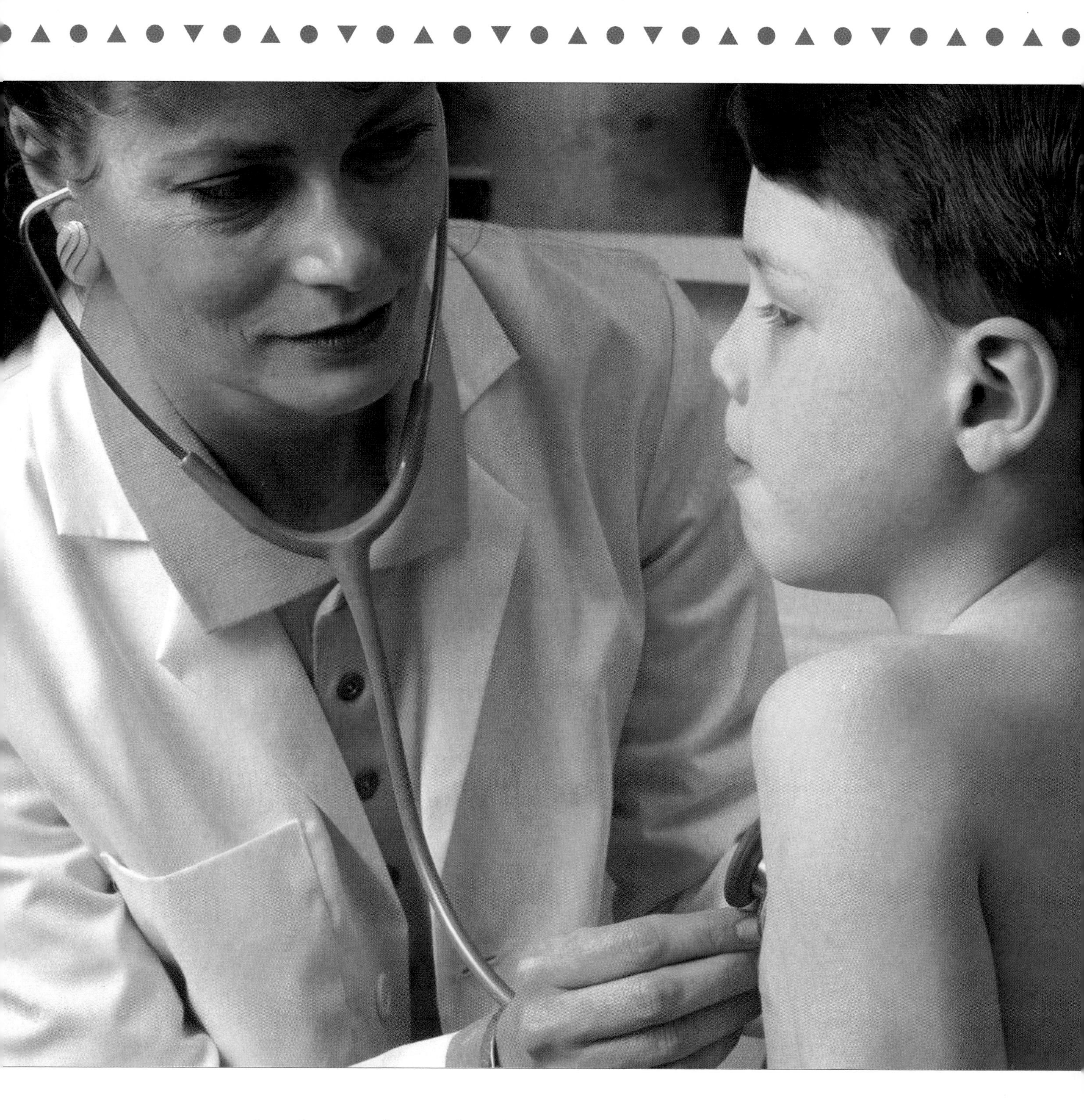

Buh-dump! Buh-dump! Your heart beats.
Whoosh! Air passes through your lungs.

The doctor looks into your throat.
The doctor also looks into your ears
and your eyes.

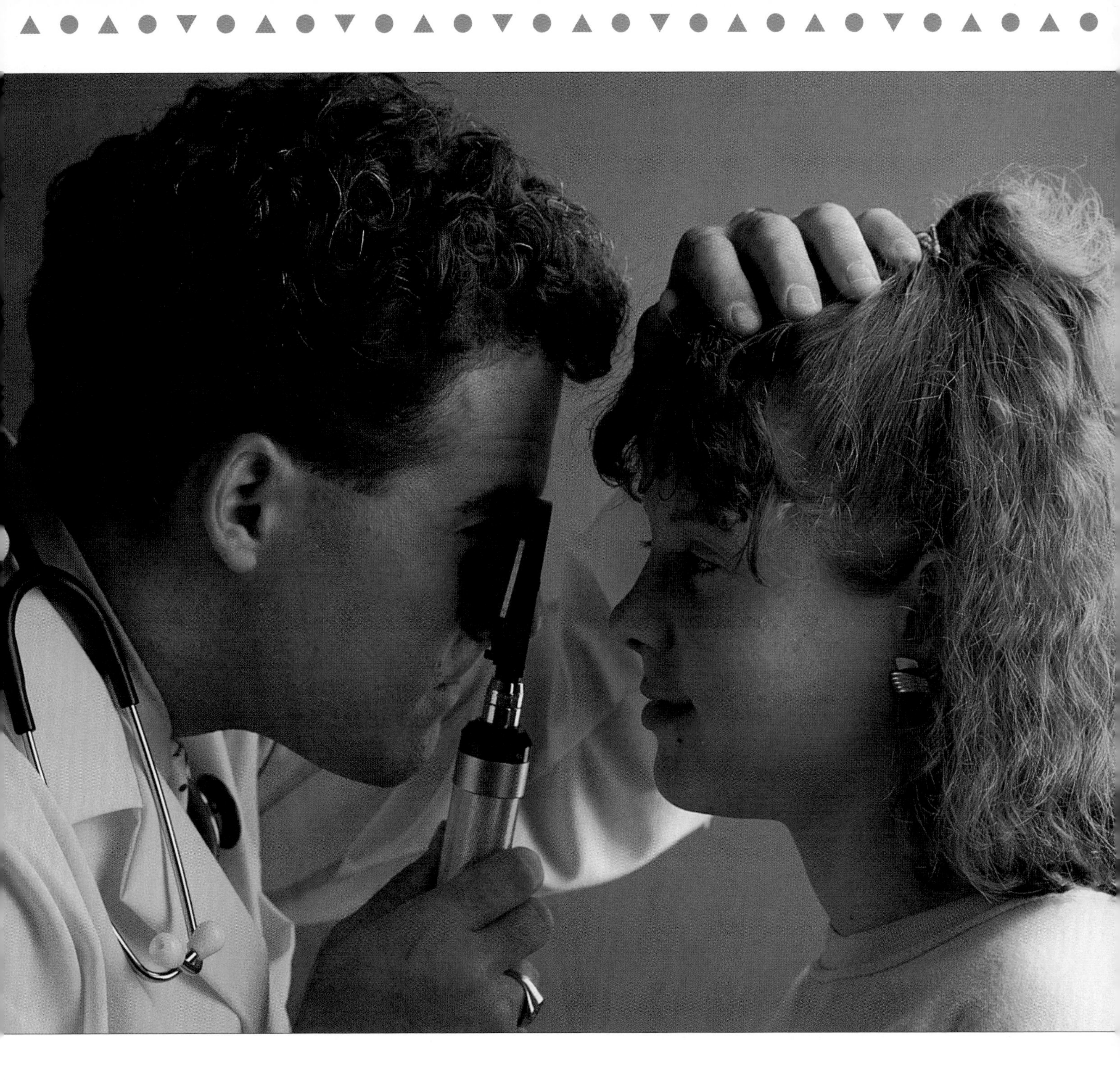

A special light helps the doctor see
inside your body.
Doctors help prevent illnesses.

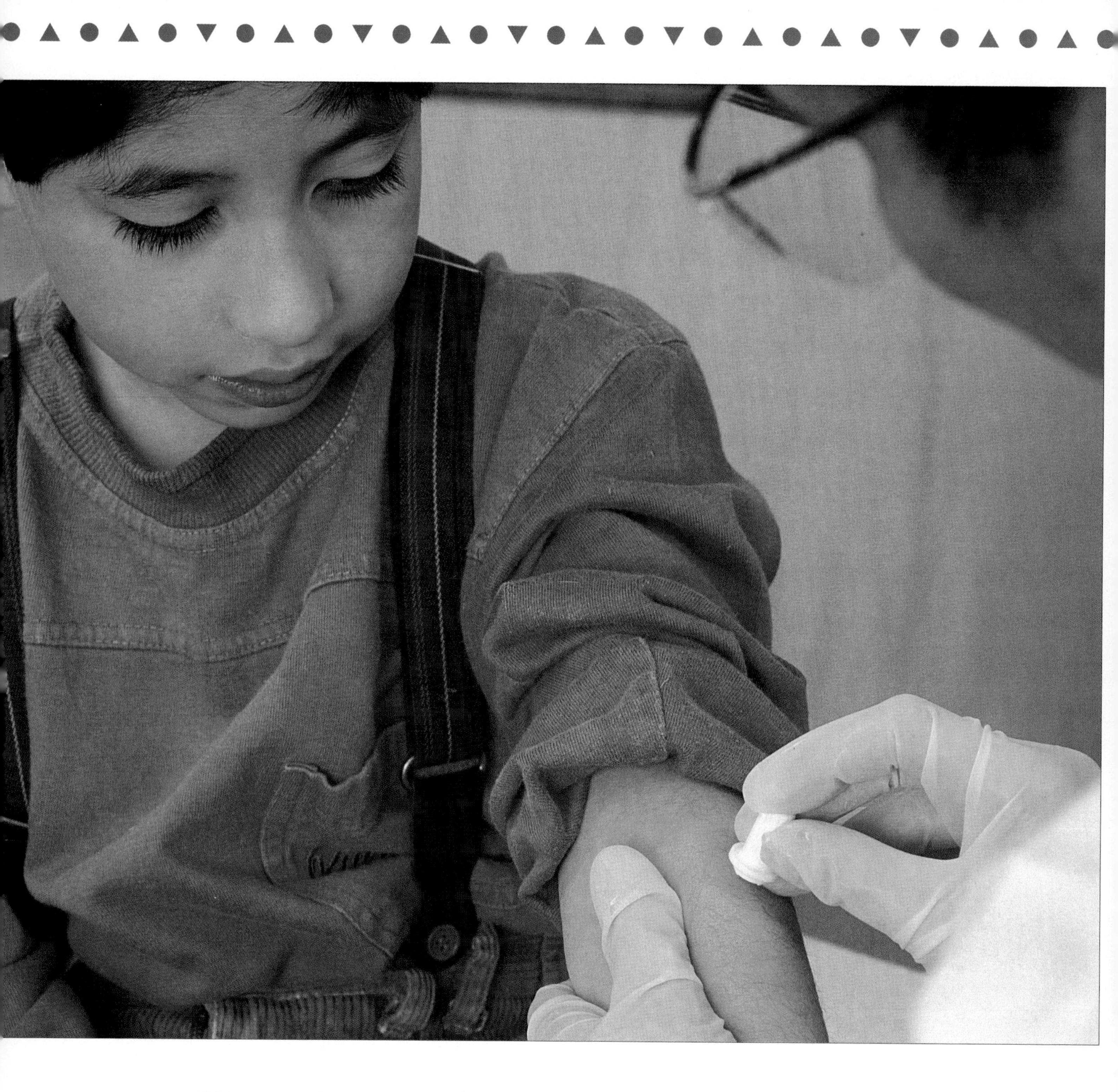

They give you shots.
These shots help your body fight off germs.
A shot may feel like a hard pinch.

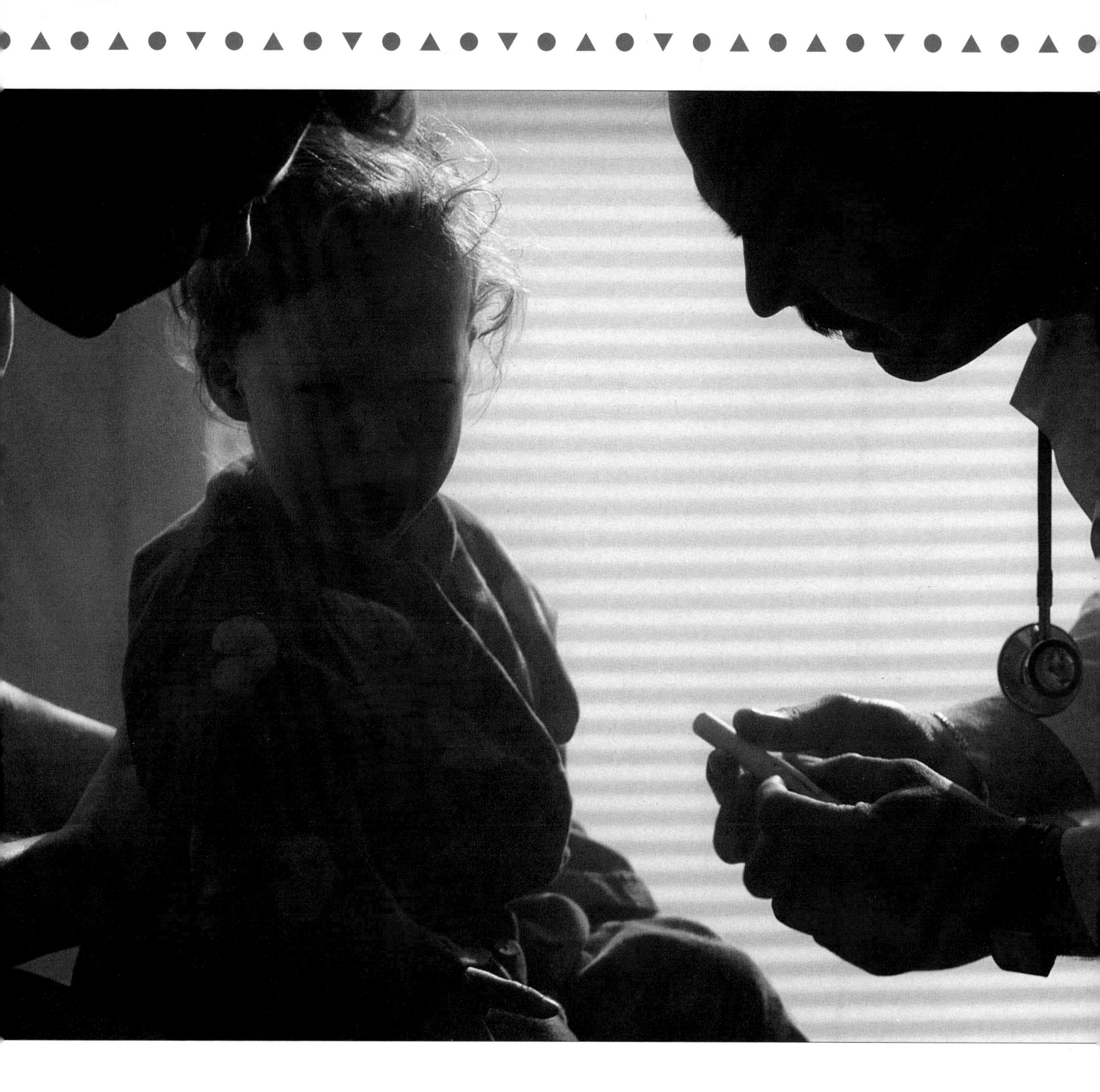

It's better to get a shot than a disease, such as polio, diphtheria, whooping cough, tetanus, measles, or mumps.

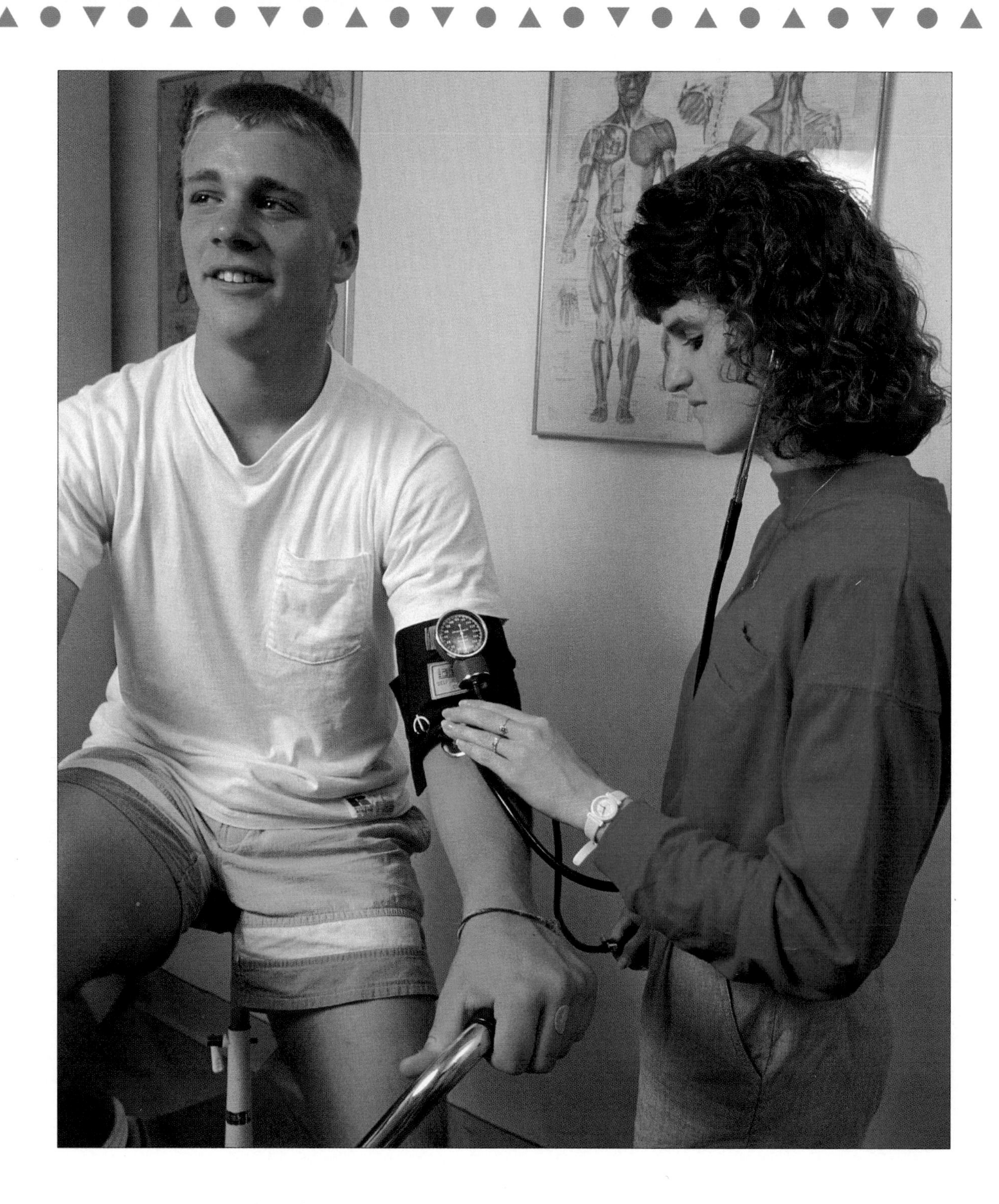

Doctors help people stay well.
They teach young and old how to eat the right foods, exercise, and get enough sleep.

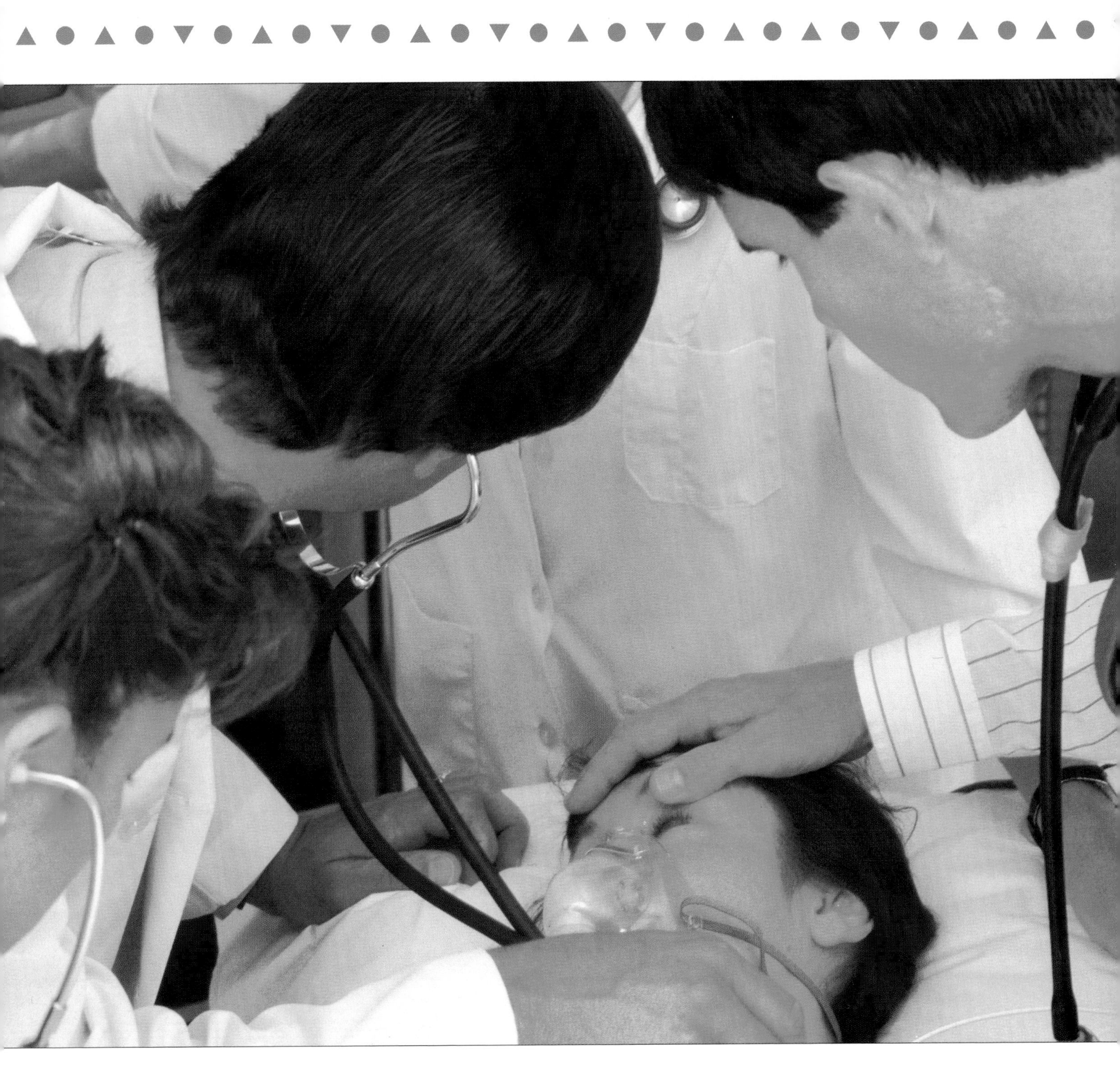

They know a strong body can fight off germs.
But even healthy people get sick sometimes.
Then your doctor will help you get better.

Do you have a scratchy, sore throat?
Does it hurt when you swallow?
Is it strep throat?

Is it tonsillitis?
Or is it just a cold?
The doctor will do some tests to find out.

Does your ear hurt?
The doctor might give you some drops
to put in the ear that hurts.

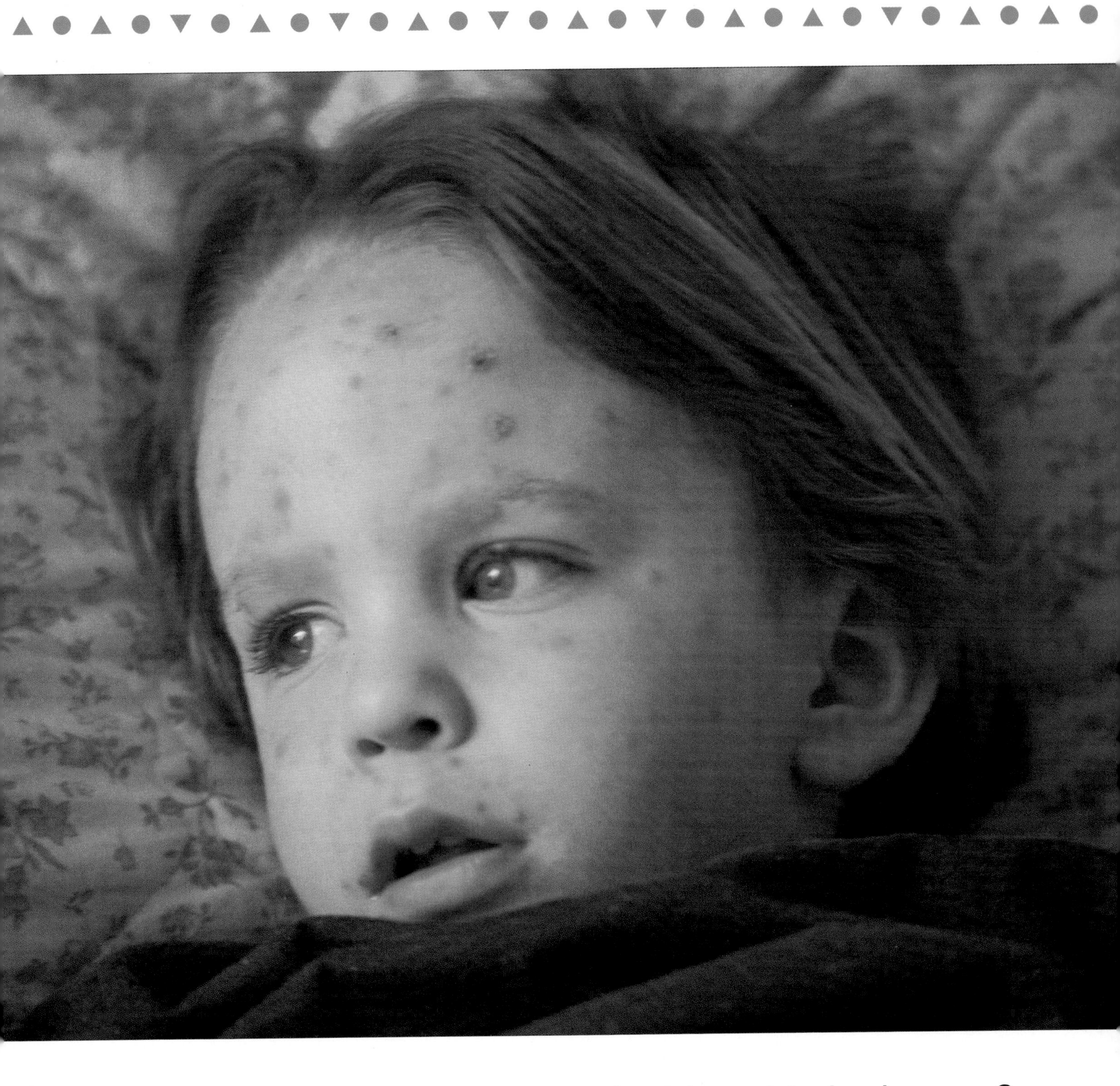

Did you wake up covered with red itchy bumps?
Is it a rash or the measles? Don't scratch.
Get to the doctor on the double!

Most of the time,
you see the doctor at the office.

But doctors also
help people in the hospital.

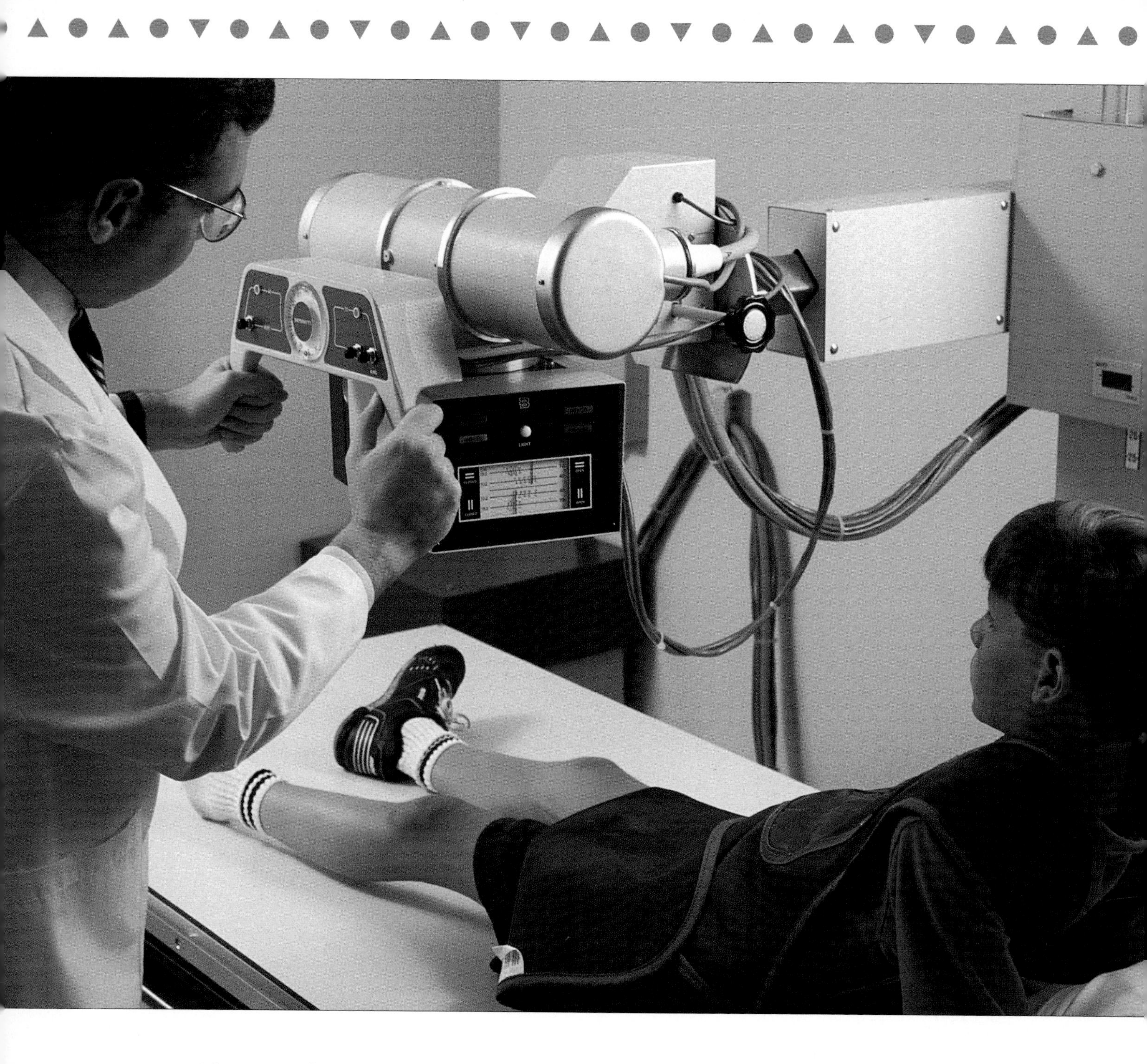

If you break your leg,
the doctor will fix it in the hospital.
A doctor is ready to take care of you every
hour of the day, every day of the week.

That's because people can get sick or have an accident anytime.
Your doctor is always learning better ways to care for you.

The more doctors know about the body, the better they can find new ways to keep you healthy. Do you know that you can help your doctor?

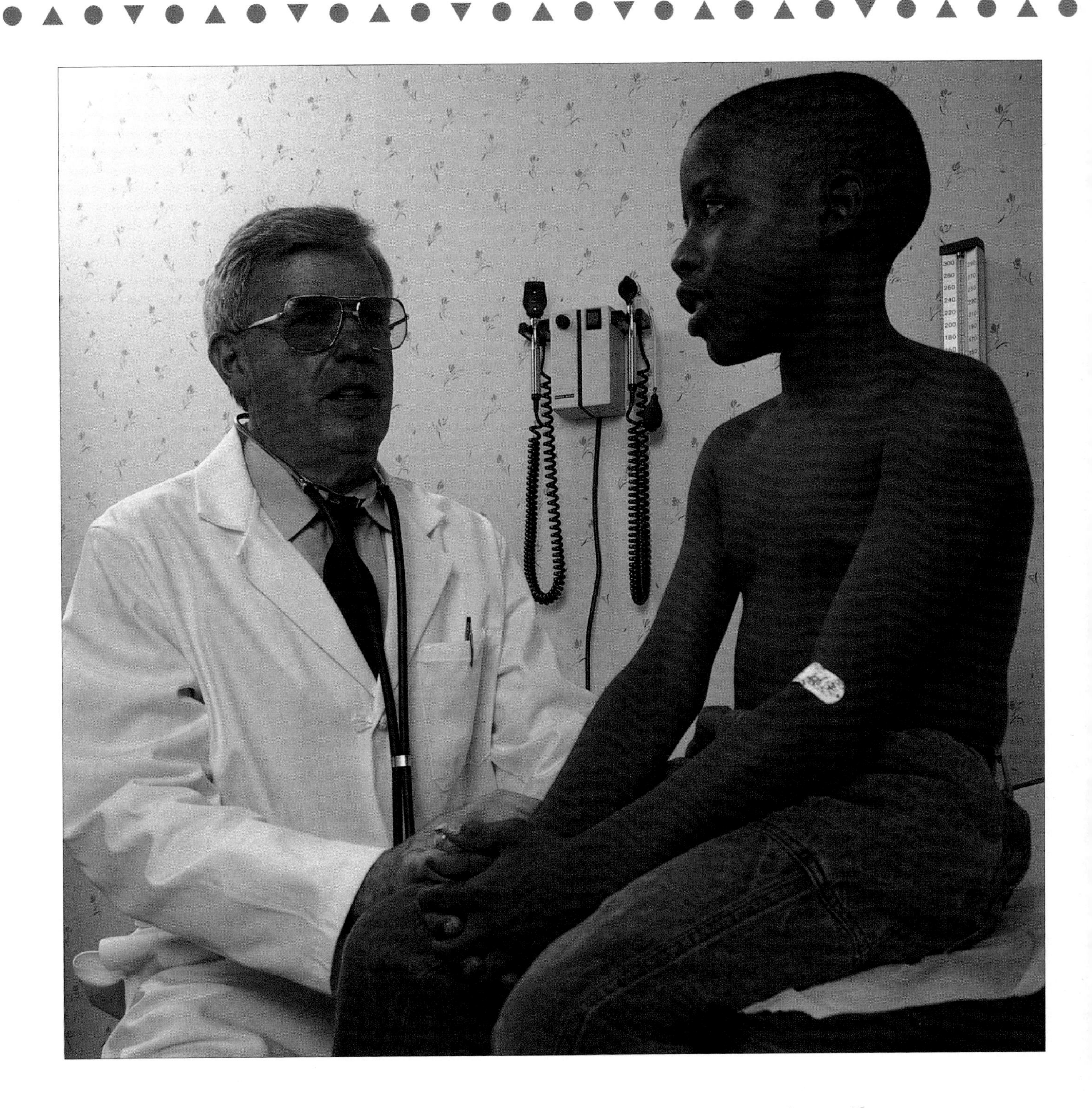

You can help by talking about your family.
You can help by telling exactly how you feel.
You can help by asking questions.

You have an important job when you see the doctor. You can teach the doctor all about you!

Questions and Answers

How does a person become a doctor?

Most people go to college for four years. They study biology and science and get a bachelor's degree. Then they take a special test called the Medical College Admissions Test (MCAT). This test checks the person's understanding of chemistry, biology, and physics. It checks how well the person can read and think about things. The test is hard and long. It takes seven hours to finish the MCAT examination. If a person passes the test they can go to medical school for four more years.

What does a person do in medical school?

In medical school, the students learn from books and other doctors. They also begin to work with sick people. They learn to listen carefully to the answers sick people give them. After they graduate from medical school, they work in a hospital for a year. And if they want to be a special kind of doctor, like a pediatrician, they have to train for another three years! That's twelve years altogether.

Do all doctors work with sick people?

No. some doctors become teachers. They teach classes at medical schools. Other doctors do research for businesses, the government, hospitals, or universities.

How many hours a day do doctors work?

In the morning, some doctors see patients in the hospital. In the afternoon they may treat patients in the office. In between, they talk to patients on the phone.

GLOSSARY

blood—a liquid pumped through the body by the heart that carries oxygen and other good things

blood pressure—the amount of force used by the heart to pump blood

checkup—a physical examination given by a doctor

disease—a sickness that is caused by germs or a break down of how the body works

earache—a pain in the ear

flu—a sickness caused by germs

germs—things too small to be seen that carry disease

healthy—being in good health without sickness or pain

heart—the part of the body used to pump blood

hospital—a place built to help people who are sick or hurt

lungs—the part of the body that moves oxygen in and out of the body

measure—to count or find out how long or big something is

pediatrician—a doctor trained to take care of young children

shot—a liquid medicine given with a needle

stethoscope—a tool used by doctors to listen to the sounds the body makes

temperature—how hot or cold something is

▲ ● ▼ ● ▲ ● ▼ ● ▲ ● ▼

AMY MOSES writes books for children, teachers, and parents. She earned her master's degree in education with a Specialty in Reading. Amy is currently writing a novel. She loves reading, writing, making things, and being outdoors.

W9-BYZ-043

SAM GARTON

BALZER + BRAY

An Imprint of HarperCollins*Publishers*

This book is for everyone
who loves Otter.

Balzer + Bray is an imprint of HarperCollins Publishers.

I Am Otter

For information address HarperCollins Children's Books, a division of HarperCollins Publishers, 10 East 53rd Street, New York, NY 10022.
www.harpercollinschildrens.com

Library of Congress Cataloging-in-Publication Data
Garton, Sam, author, illustrator.
I am Otter / by Sam Garton. — First edition.
pages cm
Summary: Otter decides to open a toast restaurant with her best friend, Teddy, but after she blames Teddy for the mess they made, he goes missing.
ISBN 978-0-06-224775-9
[1. Otters—Fiction. 2. Teddy bears—Fiction. 3. Friendship—Fiction. 4. Lost and found possessions—Fiction.] I. Title.
PZ7.G211716 Iam 2012043482
[E]—dc23 CIP
AC

The artist used Adobe Photoshop to create the digital illustrations for this book.
Typography by Dana Fritts
13 14 15 16 17 SCP 10 9 8 7 6 5 4 3 2 1
❖
First Edition

Hi! I am Otter.
No one really knows where I came
from. Otter Keeper says that he found
me in a box on his doorstep one day.

He says back then I was very small. I'm still quite small, so I must have been really tiny. I wish I'd made the most of being that little.

At first I was a bit scared of Otter Keeper.
But luckily, Teddy had just come to live
with Otter Keeper too.

Now I love Otter Keeper and Teddy very much. We have so much fun together, you wouldn't believe it!

Especially on the weekends.

But then every Monday we get bad news:
Otter Keeper will be going to work.

I do all sorts of things to prevent
Otter Keeper from leaving, like
trying to stop Monday
from happening altogether,

or hiding his lunch where
he'll never find it.

But my plans never work.

Teddy and I think it is very unfair that we don't have jobs. So one day we decided to start our own business: a toast restaurant!

After some
basic training . . .

we opened for business.

Right away, though, we ran into problems.

First, Teddy had forgotten to take the reservations.

Next, Teddy hadn't told anyone how much our toast would cost. As a result, no one brought any spending money, which led to some embarrassing situations.

Finally, Teddy got several of the toast orders wrong.

Some of the customers complained and had to be asked to leave the restaurant.

That was the last straw. So Teddy was fired and I gave his job to Giraffe.

But even with a new chef, the restaurant still had big problems.

SAUCE
Baking

tost reStrA
open
CLOSd
ples go home. now.
Strawberry
Heat

But the biggest problem of all was:
Otter Keeper had just come home!

Everyone had to hide!

Luckily, Otters are very good at hiding.

Unluckily, Otter Keepers are very good at finding Otters.

The toast restaurant was shut down. Things had to be cleaned up. And everyone was sent home.

I tried to explain to Otter Keeper
that this had all been Teddy's fault.

But wait . . . where *was* Teddy?

I'd been so mean to Teddy, he'd probably run away to start a new toast restaurant with someone else.

At bedtime, Teddy still hadn't turned up. And I couldn't sleep.

This was an

emergency!

Luckily, in an emergency, you are allowed to wake up Otter Keeper.

The search began. . . .

After hunting almost all night,

we were running out
of places to look.

Then all of a sudden I had
a clever thought. . . .

Teddy!
TOYS

Now everything is normal again.

Otter Keeper still goes to work.

But I don't mind as much, because
I have my best friend back.

And now, when things go wrong, I understand
they are not actually Teddy's fault at all.

They are Giraffe’s.